NATIVE AMERICAN PEOPLES

INVESTIGATE!

THE CHEROKEE

Enslow PUBLISHING

BY JOHN O'MARA

Please visit our website, www.enslow.com. For a free color catalog of all our high-quality books, call toll free 1-800-398-2504 or fax 1-877-980-4454.

Library of Congress Cataloging-in-Publication Data
Names: O'Mara, John, author.
Title: The Cherokee / John O'Mara.
Other titles: Native American peoples.
Description: New York : Enslow Publishing, [2022] | Series: Native American peoples | Includes index.
Identifiers: LCCN 2020028573 (print) | LCCN 2020028574 (ebook) | ISBN 9781978521803 (library binding) | ISBN 9781978521780 (paperback) | ISBN 9781978521797 (set) | ISBN 9781978521810 (ebook)
Subjects: LCSH: Cherokee Indians–Juvenile literature. | Cherokee Indians–History–Juvenile literature.
Classification: LCC E99.C5 O53 2022 (print) | LCC E99.C5 (ebook) | DDC 975.004/97557–dc23
LC record available at https://lccn.loc.gov/2020028573
LC ebook record available at https://lccn.loc.gov/2020028574

Published in 2022 by
Enslow Publishing
29 E. 21st Street
New York, NY 10010

Designer: Katelyn E. Reynolds
Interior Layout: Tanya Dellaccio
Editor: Therese Shea

Photo credits: Cover, p. 1 (texture) aopsan/Shutterstock.com; cvr, pp. 1–24 (striped texture) Eky Studio/Shutterstock.com; p. 5 (both), 27 (right), 29 (left) George Rose/Getty Images News/Getty Images; pp. 6, 9 (top) PeterHermesFurian/iStock/Getty Images Plus/Getty Images; p. 9 (bottom) Cavan Images/Cavan/Getty Images; p. 11 (left) RodClementPhotography/Shutterstock.com; p. 11 (right) Fotosearch/Getty Images; p. 12 Marilyn Angel Wynn/Corbis/Getty Images; p. 13 (left) Culture Club/Hulton Archive/Getty Images; p. 13 (right) Helen H. Richardson/Denver Post/Getty Images; p. 15 (left) Peter Turnley/Corbis Historical/Getty Images; pp. 15 (bottom), 20, 21 (left), 26 Bettmann/Getty Images; pp. 16, 17 Hulton Archive/Getty Images; p. 18 https://upload.wikimedia.org/wikipedia/commons/6/66/Three_Cherokee.jpg; p. 19 Interim Archives/Archive Photos/Getty Images; p. 21 (right) Library of Congress/Corbis Historical/Getty Images; p. 23 Michael Maslan/Corbis Historical/Getty Images; pp. 25 (top), 27 (left) Education Images/Universal Images Group/Getty Images; p. 29 (middle) https://upload.wikimedia.org/wikipedia/commons/b/b4/Eastern_Band_Cherokee_Flag.svg; p. 29 (right) https://upload.wikimedia.org/wikipedia/commons/f/f9/Seal_of_the_United_Keetoowah_Band_of_Cherokee_Indians.jpg.

Portions of this work were originally authored by Sarah Machajewski and published as *The Cherokee People*. All new material this edition authored by John O'Mara.

Printed in the United States of America

CPSIA compliance information: Batch #CSENS22: For further information contact Enslow Publishing, New York, New York, at 1-800-398-2504.

CONTENTS

WORDS IN THE GLOSSARY APPEAR IN **BOLD** TYPE THE FIRST TIME THEY ARE USED IN THE TEXT.

A RESILIENT PEOPLE

The Native American tribe called the Cherokee Nation is the largest native group in the United States. More than 370,000 people are members of the Cherokee Nation. There are other groups of Cherokee too. In addition, hundreds of thousands of people have Cherokee **ancestors**!

The amazing people who call themselves Cherokee have a history that goes back thousands of years. It's a story of **tradition**, hardship, loss, and **resilience**. Learning about the past of this native people is a way to show respect for their great **culture**.

GET THE FACTS!

The Cherokee speak a language from the Iroquois family of Native American languages. There were about 16 Iroquois languages in all, including Cherokee, Mohawk, and Seneca. Some of the Iroquois languages are extinct, which means no one speaks them anymore.

TODAY'S CHEROKEE PEOPLE LIVE MUCH LIKE OTHER AMERICANS. STILL, THEY HONOR AND REMEMBER THEIR CULTURE IN MANY WAYS.

THE CHEROKEE'S ORIGINS

Historians think all Native Americans are **descended** from people who crossed from Asia into North America. This probably happened more than 15,000 years ago. At that time, a land bridge existed between the areas. It's now covered by water.

ALASKA IS SEPARATED FROM RUSSIA BY A CHANNEL OF WATER CALLED THE BERING STRAIT. THE STRAIT WASN'T COVERED BY WATER AT ONE TIME, ALLOWING PEOPLE TO TRAVEL OVER IT.

GET THE FACTS!

The area between Russia and Canada, including Alaska, is called Beringia. Land appeared there after the sea levels dropped. The land is sometimes called the Bering Land Bridge. This happened during a period on Earth when cold conditions locked seawater in glaciers.

BERING LAND BRIDGE MEASUREMENTS

- ABOUT 1,000 MILES (1,609 KM) FROM NORTH TO SOUTH
- ABOUT 3,000 MILES (4,828 KM) FROM WEST TO EAST

Groups of people slowly moved south to areas in North and South America where they could find food. They settled in different places. Over time, they lost contact with each other. That's how so many peoples, such as the Cherokee, formed their special cultures, which included different languages and traditions.

Around 10,000 years ago, the ancestors of the Cherokee settled in the Appalachian Mountains in today's southeastern United States. Their villages were on land that became the states of Kentucky, West Virginia, Virginia, North Carolina, South Carolina, Georgia, Alabama, and Tennessee. Today, most Cherokee people live in Oklahoma. Another large group lives in North Carolina.

The Creek, another native people, may have provided the name most use for the Cherokee. "Cherokee" likely comes from a Creek word meaning "people of different speech." Europeans used this name for the Cherokee people.

GET THE FACTS!

Long ago, the Cherokee called themselves *Aniyunwiya*, which means "principal people." This word is spelled in many ways. Now, most use the name Cherokee for themselves. However, the right way to say and spell Cherokee in their own language is *Tsalagi*.

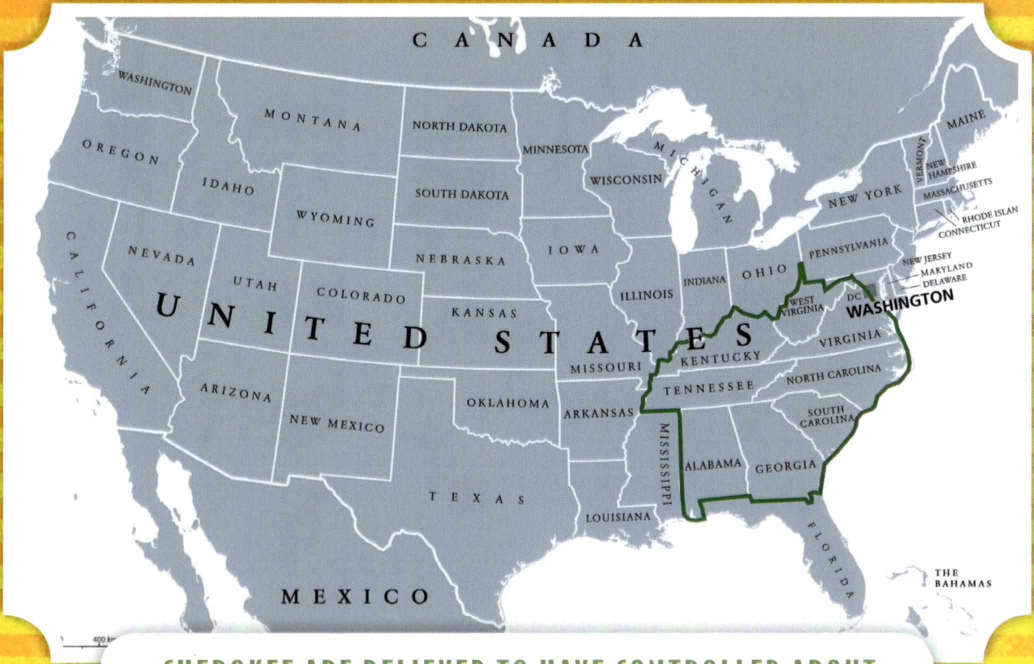

CHEROKEE ARE BELIEVED TO HAVE CONTROLLED ABOUT 40,000 SQUARE MILES (104,000 SQ KM) IN THE 1600s.

ORIGINAL CHEROKEE HOMELANDS

- TENNESSEE
- NORTH CAROLINA
- SOUTH CAROLINA
- KENTUCKY
- WEST VIRGINIA
- VIRGINIA
- GEORGIA
- ALABAMA

APPALACHIAN MOUNTAINS (SMOKY MOUNTAIN RANGE)

HOMES THEN AND NOW

The Cherokee had two kinds of homes, often next to each other. In summer, they lived in homes of mud, clay, and wood. Their winter homes were sunk into the ground for warmth. The roof of grass and clay could be as thick as 7 inches (18 cm). The houses were large to fit big families.

GET THE FACTS!

About 30 to 60 houses made up a Cherokee village, and about 200 Cherokee people lived in a village. Each village had a **council** house where meetings and important events were held. Villages were often located near rivers.

THE CHEROKEE USED THINGS THEY FOUND IN NATURE TO BUILD THEIR HOMES.

Today's Cherokee people live in homes like the ones found in modern neighborhoods. Many live on reservations. Reservations are independent communities governed by Native Americans. They have houses, schools, businesses, parks, and more.

WHO WERE THE THREE SISTERS?

Nearly all Cherokee meals included corn, beans, and squash. These crops were known as the "three sisters" because they were so important to many native peoples, including the Cherokee. Each crop helped the other two grow.

The Cherokee's Green Corn **Ceremony** was celebrated when the first corn ripened. The celebration included playing sports, praying, and performing special dances.

THE THREE SISTERS

CHEROKEE DRESSED FOR THE CORN DANCE

MANY CHEROKEE CELEBRATE OLD TRADITIONS BY PREPARING THE FOODS THEIR ANCESTORS ATE AND PERFORMING THE SAME CEREMONIES.

GET THE FACTS!

The Cherokee made their own **medicine** out of plants. The bark of the black gum tree was made into a tea for people who had chest pains. The plants called cattails and hummingbird blossoms were used for other conditions.

The Cherokee also ate a lot of meat. They hunted wild animals and caught fish. They gathered nuts, berries, and roots from forests. These were used to make soups, cornbread, and more.

CHEROKEE LIFE

Cherokee men and women had different roles, but both had power. Men were the hunters and warriors. Cherokee women farmed and owned the houses and fields. They also decided whom to marry.

The Cherokee people had ceremonies for different parts of their lives. The Cherokee stomp dance honors the Creator, called Unetlanvhi, and is still practiced today. The stomp dance is performed around a fire. Dancers called "shell-shakers" wear noisemaking objects around their legs. These may be pebble-filled cans. The noise helps the performers keep the beat of the dance.

TODAY, WOMEN AND MEN CAN BE CHEROKEE CHIEFS. WILMA MANKILLER MADE HISTORY WHEN SHE BECAME THE FIRST FEMALE CHIEF OF THE CHEROKEE NATION IN 1985.

GET THE FACTS!

When Cherokee villages were at war, they had a war chief. When they were at peace, a peace chief was in charge. This chief made decisions with the help of a council of village leaders. They met and made announcements in the council house.

CHEROKEE WOMAN WEAVING BASKET

EUROPEANS MAKE CONTACT

In 1540, Spanish explorer Hernando de Soto was the first European to make contact with the Cherokee. Others followed. It's thought that the Cherokee population was about 25,000 back then. Soon, large numbers of Europeans came to settle in North America. England established several colonies where the Cherokee lived. This changed the Cherokee culture forever.

AUSTENACO WAS A CHEROKEE CHIEF IN THE 1700s. THIS WAS A TIME WHEN THE CHEROKEE WERE OFTEN AT ODDS WITH THE EUROPEAN SETTLERS AROUND THEM.

1540
CHEROKEE'S FIRST CONTACT WITH EUROPEANS

GET THE FACTS!

Europeans brought illnesses to the Cherokee and other Native American peoples that they had never had before. The illnesses killed millions. It's believed that up to 95 percent of all native peoples died in the 150 years after Christopher Columbus's arrival in 1492.

The Cherokee traded with the British. They exchanged animal furs for European guns, pots, knives, and other tools. These made parts of the Cherokee's lives easier, but some of their traditional ways began to die out.

FIGHTING FOR LAND

White settlers in North America wanted land. Some simply tried to take it from Native Americans, including the Cherokee. Many settlers viewed Native Americans as **uncivilized**, so they treated them unfairly. Fighting sometimes occurred between settlers and Cherokee.

IN 1762, THREE CHEROKEE LEADERS WERE TAKEN TO ENGLAND TO CREATE PEACE BETWEEN THE BRITISH AND THE CHEROKEE.

GET THE FACTS!

In 1758, white settlers in Virginia killed Cherokee warriors returning from the French and Indian War. In return, Cherokee attacked white settlers in North Carolina. These events began what's called the Cherokee War or the Anglo-Cherokee War, which lasted until 1761.

In 1763, the British government set a border to stop settlers from moving onto Native American land west of the Appalachian Mountains. This included Cherokee land. However, even this act, called the Proclamation of 1763, didn't stop settlers. By 1783, the United States won freedom from Great Britain. British laws were no longer in effect.

ASSIMILATING TO SURVIVE

Many Cherokee hoped assimilating, or becoming more like, white people would make white Americans treat them with respect. The Cherokee had worn clothing such as animal-skin leggings and skirts, beaded belts, and moccasins. By the end of the 1700s, most Cherokee had given these up for pants, jackets, dresses, skirts, and shoes white people wore.

ABOUT 2,500 PEOPLE SPEAK CHEROKEE WELL TODAY. THOUSANDS MORE ARE TRYING TO LEARN.

GET THE FACTS!

In the early 1800s, a Cherokee man named Sequoyah created a writing system called the Cherokee syllabary (right). Nearly all Cherokee learned how to read and write using it. It's not an alphabet. Rather, it's 85 characters that stand for sounds used to speak Cherokee.

Cherokee society also changed greatly. Tribes formed governments modeled after the United States government and adopted their own constitutions, or sets of laws. The Cherokee practiced the same **religions** as white people and created schools too.

GOLD DISCOVERY

Even with some Native Americans assimilating, territory continued to be taken from them. Between 1805 and 1832, the state of Georgia seized land from the Cherokee and Creek and gave it to white settlers. In addition, in summer 1829, a newspaper announced gold was found in Cherokee territory in Georgia. By winter, thousands of miners arrived to try to strike it rich.

Cherokee fought for their rights in the U.S. Supreme Court, the highest court in the nation. In 1832, the court decided Georgia state law didn't apply to Cherokee territory.

GET THE FACTS!

In 1832, the Chief Justice of the United States, John Marshall, stated that Cherokee land was a separate community from the state of Georgia. So, state law didn't have power in Cherokee land. Only the federal government could have dealings with Native Americans.

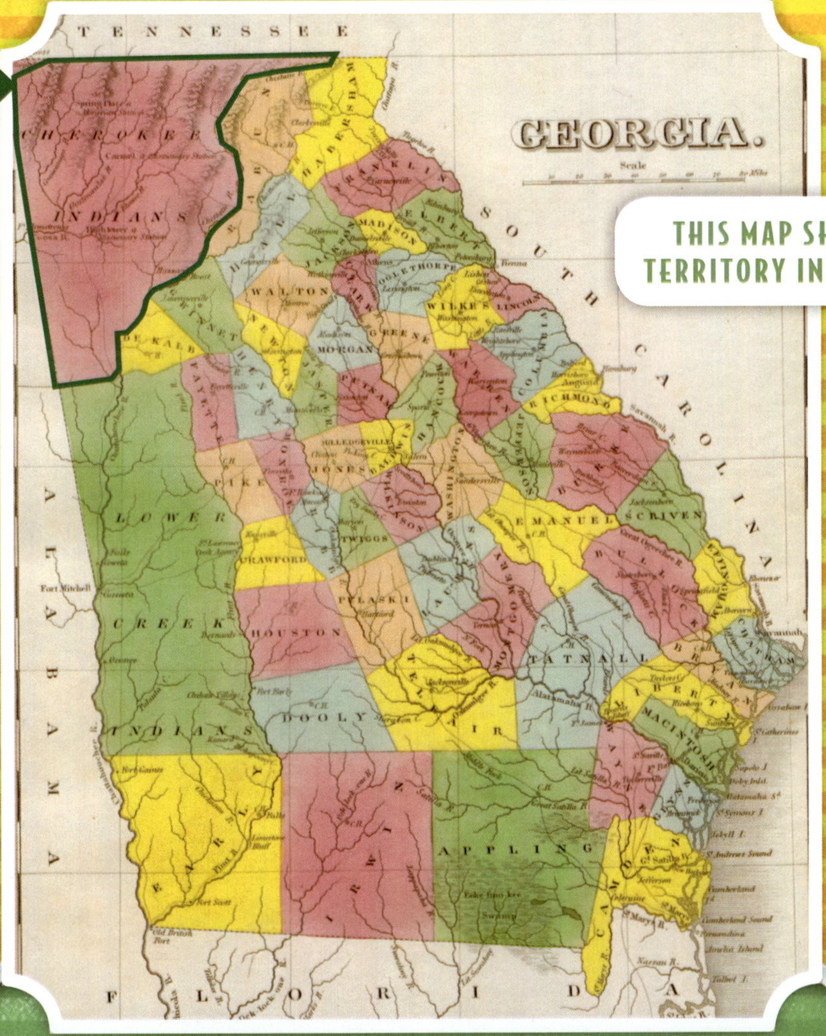

THIS MAP SHOWS CHEROKEE TERRITORY IN GEORGIA IN 1826.

THE INDIAN REMOVAL ACT

In 1830, President Andrew Jackson signed the Indian Removal Act. This allowed the government to push Native Americans off their lands. Some accepted money for their territory. Others, including most Cherokee, refused to move.

In the winter of 1838–1839, U.S. soldiers forced the Cherokee to move. Men, women, and children traveled more than 1,000 miles (1,609 km) to a reservation in what was called Indian Territory, today's Oklahoma. Over 4,000 Cherokee died on the way. The forced removal of the Native Americans of the Southeast is known as the Trail of Tears.

TRAIL OF TEARS ROUTES

ABOUT 5,045 MILES (8,119 KM)

STATES: ALABAMA, ARKANSAS, GEORGIA, ILLINOIS, KENTUCKY, MISSOURI, NORTH CAROLINA, OKLAHOMA, TENNESSEE

TODAY, THE TRAIL OF TEARS NATIONAL HISTORIC TRAIL HELPS US REMEMBER THIS TERRIBLE PART OF U.S. HISTORY.

GET THE FACTS!

Why was the Trail of Tears so deadly? Many Cherokee were forced to travel in the winter without shelter or clothing, sometimes even without shoes. There wasn't enough food, and the Cherokee weren't allowed to stop when they were ill.

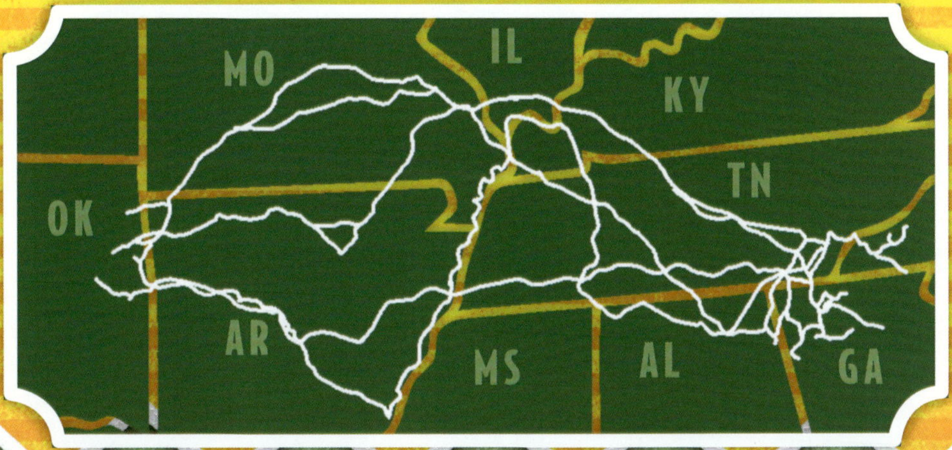

THE CHEROKEE TRAIL OF TEARS WASN'T JUST ONE ROUTE WEST, AS THIS MAP SHOWS.

REBUILDING THEIR NATION

After the Trail of Tears, it took many years to rebuild Cherokee society. One-fourth of the Cherokee Nation had died on their journey west. There were years of unrest between Cherokee who had agreed to move to Indian Territory and those who had fought against it. The Cherokee people were again divided during the **American Civil War**. Thousands lost their lives.

GET THE FACTS!

A few hundred Cherokee escaped before they could be rounded up and forced to march west. U.S. soldiers couldn't find them in the mountains of North Carolina. People descended from these Cherokee live in western North Carolina today as the Eastern Band of Cherokee Indians.

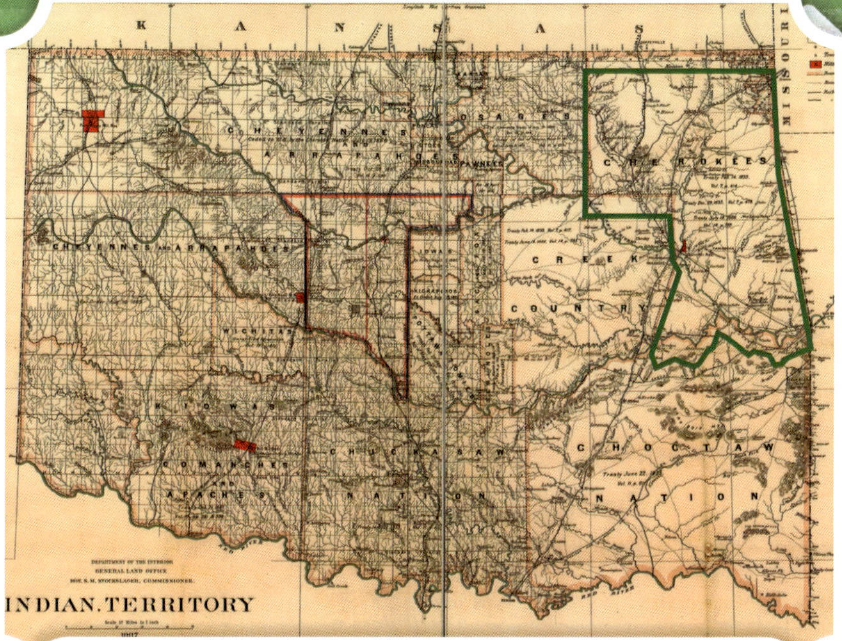

PART OF INDIAN TERRITORY WAS OPENED TO WHITE SETTLERS IN 1889. IT BECAME THE TERRITORY OF OKLAHOMA. THE TWO PARTS JOINED AGAIN AND BECAME THE STATE OF OKLAHOMA IN 1907.

However, the Cherokee managed to establish themselves in Indian Territory. They formed new governments, farms, schools, and businesses. Many became successful leaders, farmers, ranchers, teachers, businesspeople, and artists.

TODAY'S CHEROKEE PEOPLE

The federal government recognizes three groups of Cherokee people today. They are the Cherokee Nation, the United Keetoowah Band of Cherokee Indians, and the Eastern Band of Cherokee Indians. However, there are other groups in Georgia, Alabama, and other places.

GET THE FACTS!

The United Keetoowah Band of Cherokee Indians is located in Oklahoma, like the Cherokee Nation. They believe *Keetoowah* or *Kituwah* is the real name of the Cherokee people. Their ancestors moved west years before the Trail of Tears happened.

CHEROKEE TODAY PASS DOWN THEIR VALUES, INCLUDING THE IMPORTANCE OF FAMILY, FRIENDSHIP, AND PRIDE AS A PEOPLE.

The Cherokee still work hard to protect their culture. They educate Cherokee children and others about their ways of life in the hope that they will continue them. Their history is full of examples of their resilience against opposition. The Cherokee are a strong people with a bright future.

GLOSSARY

American Civil War A war fought from 1861 to 1865 in the United States between the Union (the Northern states) and the Confederacy (the Southern states).

ancestor A relative who lived long before you.

ceremony An event to honor or celebrate something.

council A group of people meant to make decisions for a bigger group.

culture The beliefs and ways of life of a group of people.

descended Coming long after another in a family.

French and Indian War A war between Great Britain and France in North America, fought from 1754 to 1763.

medicine A drug taken to make a sick person well.

religion A belief in and way of honoring a god or gods.

resilience The ability to become successful again after bad events happen.

tradition A long-practiced custom.

uncivilized Not having a high level of culture.

FOR MORE INFORMATION

BOOKS

Bodden, Valerie. *Cherokee*. Mankato, MN: Creative Education/ Creative Paperbacks, 2018.

Nelson, Kristen Rajczak. *The Trail of Tears: A Journey of Loss.* New York, NY: Lucent Press, 2018.

Roberts, Russell. *The Cherokee*. Kennett Square, PA: Purple Toad Publishing, 2016.

WEBSITES

Cherokee Indian Fact Sheet
www.bigorrin.org/cherokee_kids.htm
Read short questions and answers about Cherokee history.

Cherokee Nation
www.cherokee.org
Read about the Cherokee Nation today.

INDEX